What Is the Story of Willy Wonka?

by Steve Korté

illustrated by Jake Murray

Penguin Workshop

For Naomi and Eli—SK

For all the art, music, and literature teachers
who encourage us to discover wonderful
worlds of pure imagination!—JM

PENGUIN WORKSHOP
An Imprint of Penguin Random House LLC, New York

**ROALD
DAHL**

www.roalddahl.com

©2021 The Roald Dahl Story Company Ltd.
Published by Penguin Workshop, an imprint of Penguin Random House LLC, New York.
PENGUIN and PENGUIN WORKSHOP are trademarks of Penguin Books Ltd.
WHO HQ & Design is a registered trademark of Penguin Random House LLC.
Printed in the USA.

Visit us online at www.penguinrandomhouse.com.

Library of Congress Cataloging-in-Publication Data is available upon request.

ISBN 9780593224205 (paperback)   10 9 8 7 6 5 4 3 2
ISBN 9780593224212 (library binding)   10 9 8 7 6 5 4 3 2 1

Contents

What Is the Story of Willy Wonka?

The big day had finally arrived! At the edge of town, there stood a giant chocolate factory. It was the Wonka Factory, and it was the largest and most famous chocolate and candy factory in the world.

The factory was owned by a mysterious man named Willy Wonka. Wonka was called "the most *fantastic*, the most *extraordinary* chocolate maker the world has ever seen!" What no one could figure out, though, was how his factory produced its amazing candy. The huge iron gates to the Wonka Factory had been locked shut for the past decade. No employees were seen entering or leaving the building. No one had seen Willy Wonka himself for years. But that was about to change.

On February 1, the gates were going to open for five *very* lucky children. All five had been promised a tour of the factory that was going to be led by Willy Wonka himself. The children were told that they were about to experience "mystic and marvelous surprises that will entrance,

delight, intrigue, astonish, and perplex you beyond measure. In your wildest dreams you could not imagine that such things could happen to you!"

The biggest surprise of all, though, was a secret that only Willy Wonka himself knew.

The story of Willy Wonka and his chocolate factory, written by Roald Dahl, has been a best seller for decades. It has inspired two feature films and a stage musical that has been performed around the world. And it introduced the world to Willy Wonka, one of the most memorable characters in children's literature.

CHAPTER 1
Growing Up

The man who created Willy Wonka was named Roald Dahl. He was born in Wales on September 13, 1916, to Norwegian parents. Roald's mother read bedtime stories to him, and he especially loved to hear old Norwegian fairy tales that were filled with monsters and trolls and other fantastic creatures.

When Roald was three, one of his older sisters died. A few months after that, his father died. Roald's mother was forced to care for six children on her own, but she kept her loving family together.

Roald started attending school in the town of Llandaff in Wales when he was seven years old. Every day, as he and his friends traveled to and

from school, they would stop in front of a local candy store. Roald and his friends all loved candy.

Years later, Roald remembered: "We lingered outside its rather small window gazing in at the big glass jars full of Bull's-eyes and Old Fashioned Humbugs and Strawberry Bonbons and Glacier Mints and Acid Drops and Pear Drops and Lemon Drops and all the rest of them.

My own favorites were Sherbet Suckers and Liquorice Bootlaces." These were the fantastic names of the types of candy available in Wales in the early twentieth century.

Unfortunately, the owner of the candy store was a very mean woman named Mrs. Pratchett. She had a terrible temper and was never nice to the children who came into her store.

"She never smiled," said Roald. "She never welcomed us when we went in, and the only times she spoke were when she said things like, 'I'm watchin' you so keep yer thievin' fingers off them chocolates!' "

Roald and four of his friends decided to teach Mrs. Pratchett a lesson. Roald came up with what he called the Great Mouse Plot. It involved dropping a dead mouse into a jar of Gobstopper candies in her store. Gobstoppers cost one penny each and were large hard round balls that were about the size of small tomatoes.

One day after school, the boys entered the shop. When Mrs. Pratchett wasn't looking, Roald lifted the glass lid of the Gobstoppers jar and dropped the mouse in it.

"I felt like a hero," said Roald. "I *was* a hero."

Unfortunately, the boys' moment of triumph didn't last long. Mrs. Pratchett went to their school the next day and demanded that the boys be punished. The headmaster of the school decided to hit all five boys hard on their rears with a wooden cane!

"When I returned to the classroom my eyes were wet with tears and everybody stared at me," remembered Roald. "My bottom hurt when I sat down at my desk."

Roald's mother was outraged when she heard about the caning. She marched over to the school and told the headmaster never to hit her son again. She also decided that Roald would attend a different school the following year.

CHAPTER 2
Boarding Schools

When Roald was nine years old, he was sent away to a boarding school in England. It was called St. Peter's Preparatory School, and he was forced to live there full-time except during the holidays when he could return home. Roald hated St. Peter's and was very homesick. One thing that made him happy, though, was writing.

"At St. Peter's, Sunday morning was letter-writing time," remembered Roald. "At nine o'clock the whole school had to go to their desks and spend one hour writing a letter home to their parents. From that very first Sunday at St. Peter's until the day my mother died thirty-two years later, I wrote to her once a

week, sometimes more often, whenever I was away from home."

Roald was so homesick during his first year at St. Peter's that he came up with a scheme to get away from the school. He faked having appendicitis. He wasn't able to fool a doctor, though, and was sent back to school.

When Roald turned thirteen, he started attending a different boarding school. This one was in Repton, England, and it turned out to be even worse than St. Peter's. At Repton School, the teachers, and even some of the other *students*, were allowed to beat Roald with a wooden cane!

Repton School

Roald hated almost everything about his life at Repton. But he did have one pleasant memory from those days. The famous Cadbury's chocolate company was located nearby, and occasionally it would send a free box of wrapped chocolates to each student in the school.

"Inside the box there were twelve bars of chocolate, all of different shapes, all with different fillings and all with numbers from one to twelve stamped on the chocolate underneath," said Roald.

Cadbury's wanted the schoolboys to rate the chocolate bars and send in their comments on why they liked or disliked each one. Roald loved eating chocolates, and he began to realize that large chocolate companies had workrooms that were like laboratories where they invented and developed all kinds of wonderful new items.

"I used to imagine myself working in one of these labs and suddenly I would come up with something so absolutely unbearably delicious that I would grab it in my hand and go rushing out of the lab and along the corridor and right into the office of the great Mr. Cadbury himself.

'I've got it Sir!' I would shout, putting the chocolate in front of him. 'It's fantastic! It's fabulous! It's marvellous! It's irresistible!'"

Almost thirty years later, those dreams would prove to be quite useful when Roald started writing *Charlie and the Chocolate Factory*.

CHAPTER 3
Becoming a Writer

Roald graduated from Repton School in 1934, and four years later, he set out to explore

Africa. He then served in England's Royal Air Force as a fighter pilot and worked as a spy during World War II. And that's not all he did. During the 1940s, Roald started writing short stories and novels for adults. He dreamed of becoming a full-time writer, but he found that it was hard to make a living doing that.

He met the filmmaker Walt Disney in 1942,

and together they started working on a movie idea about gremlins, which is what they called small imaginary creatures that caused problems for Royal Air Force pilots. The movie was never made, but the story

eventually was adapted by Roald and was called *The Gremlins*, which was published in 1943 as his first children's book.

In 1951, Roald met an American actress named Patricia Neal. Although she didn't like him at first, they eventually fell in love and got married in 1953. The couple lived together in a small apartment in New York City and also bought a house in England near Roald's mother. Five children were born between 1955 and 1965, and Roald became a devoted father.

The Gremlins

Roald Dahl's storybook *The Gremlins* was published in 1943 and featured illustrations by Walt Disney Studio artists. Eleanor Roosevelt, the wife of US president Franklin D. Roosevelt, loved the book and read it to her grandchildren.

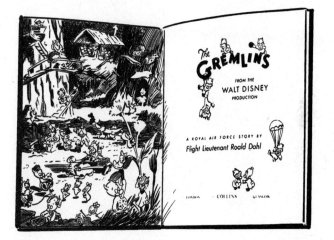

Today, a copy of the first American edition of *The Gremlins* is very valuable, sometimes selling for several thousand dollars.

Patricia Neal (1926–2010)

Patricia Neal was a stage and movie actress. She and Roald Dahl were married for thirty years. And in the early years of their marriage, it was Patricia's acting income that supported their family. Patricia won a Best Actress Academy Award—an Oscar—for her performance in the 1963 movie *Hud*. She suffered a stroke in 1965, which forced her to relearn how to walk and talk. Amazingly, she even went back to acting after her stroke and was nominated for another Best Actress Oscar for her role in the 1968 movie *The Subject Was Roses*.

Patricia and Roald divorced in 1983.

Roald loved inventing bedtime stories for his children. One of his stories inspired Roald to write his second children's book. It was called *James and the Giant Peach*, and it was published in 1961 by the American publisher Alfred A. Knopf, Inc. *James and the Giant Peach* told the story of an orphaned boy who escaped from his two cruel aunts and found a safe place to live inside an incredibly large peach. James then had many amazing adventures as he and a variety of magical garden insects traveled across the ocean inside their giant peach.

James and the Giant Peach is now a beloved classic, but at first it was not a big success. The book received excellent reviews, but during its first year it sold only 2,600 copies. Roald Dahl was discouraged by the low sales numbers and worried that it might not be worth his time to write children's books. He even said, "For all I know they may be worthless." Fortunately, he then decided to try again.

James and the Giant Peach

Roald Dahl originally considered having James travel inside a giant cherry. In the end, though, he decided that a peach was prettier and softer—plus it had a giant pit in the center. The magical insects inside the Giant Peach that traveled with James were Miss Spider, the Old-Green-Grasshopper, the Earthworm, the Glow-worm, the Ladybird, the Silkworm, and the Centipede.

Roald's imagination was definitely working overtime in 1961. That's when he came up with another fantastic tale that began life as bedtime stories for his young son Theo. It was this set of stories that eventually became *Charlie and the Chocolate Factory.*

It took several tries for Roald to get the story just right. After he wrote an early version of

the book, he gave the manuscript to his nephew Nicholas. His nephew declared that the story was "rotten and boring." Roald ended up revising the book four times. After he finished the manuscript, he gave it to his American

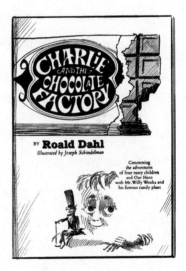

publisher. They loved it and decided to release *Charlie and the Chocolate Factory* in 1964.

CHAPTER 4
A Visit to the Chocolate Factory

Charlie and the Chocolate Factory tells the story of a little boy named Charlie Bucket, who lives with his parents and all four grandparents in a tiny, rundown house. Not far from their home is a large chocolate factory—the Wonka Factory, owned by a man named Willy Wonka. Roald described him as "the greatest inventor and maker of chocolates that there has ever been."

The huge iron gates to the chocolate factory had been locked shut for many years, and no workers were ever seen entering or leaving the building. That was because years before, spies from other candy makers had grown jealous of Willy Wonka's success.

The rival company owners had names like Slugworth, Prodnose, and Fickelgruber, and they sent spies to steal Willy Wonka's chocolate recipes.

As a result, a heartbroken Willy Wonka had to ask all his employees to leave and never come back. Once they left, the gates were locked shut.

Somehow, though, amazing chocolates and candies still emerged from the factory, packaged and ready to be sold in stores.

Charlie loved nothing more than eating a Wonka chocolate bar, but the Bucket family was so poor that they could afford to give Charlie only one chocolate bar each year for his birthday present.

Roald Dahl wrote, "The whole family saved up their money for that special occasion, and when the great day arrived, Charlie was always presented with one small chocolate bar to eat all by himself."

Then one day, something amazing happened. There was a story in the newspaper that read: "*Mr. Willy Wonka, the candy-making genius whom nobody has seen for the last ten years, sent out the following notice today*: I, Willy Wonka, have decided to allow five children—just *five*, mind you, and no more—to visit my factory this year. These lucky five will be shown around personally by me, and they will be allowed to see all the secrets and the magic of my factory. Then, at the end of the tour, as a special present, all of them will be given enough chocolates and candies to last them for the rest of their lives!"

The Daily

Mr. Willy Wonka, the candy-making genius whom nobody has seen for the last ten years, sent out the following notice today:

"I, Willy Wonka, have decided to allow five children - just five, mind you, and no more - to visit my factory this year. These lucky five will be shown around personally by me, and they will be allowed to see all the secrets and the magic of my factory. Then, at the end of the tour, as a special present, all of them will be given enough chocolates and candies to last them for the rest of their lives!"

Wonka announced that five Golden Tickets had been hidden underneath the ordinary wrapping paper of five ordinary chocolate bars that were being sent to candy shops around the world.

"The five lucky finders of these five Golden Tickets are the *only* ones who will be allowed to visit my factory and see what it's like *now* inside!" announced Willy Wonka.

Children around the world went wild trying to find those five Golden Tickets. Many, many candy bars were sold to people who were more interested in the tickets than in the chocolate. It seems as if everyone wanted the chance to go into the Wonka Factory.

Charlie's grandpa Joe said, "Wouldn't it be

something, Charlie, to open a bar of candy and see a Golden Ticket glistening inside!"

"It certainly would, Grandpa. But there isn't a hope," Charlie said sadly. "I only get one bar a year."

The first four Golden Tickets were found by some pretty awful children. Augustus Gloop was a greedy German boy who had grown very large from eating too many chocolates. Veruca Salt was a spoiled brat who screamed at her parents if they denied her anything. Violet Beauregarde spent her days and nights chewing bubblegum. Mike Teavee was a boy who spent all his time watching television.

Charlie dreamed of becoming the fifth contest winner, but he knew the odds were against him. When his birthday came, he nervously opened his yearly chocolate bar. He tore the wrapping paper right down the middle, only to discover that there was no Golden Ticket.

Then a miracle occurred. Charlie found a dollar bill buried in a snowy sidewalk gutter. He took that dollar bill to the candy store and purchased one of Wonka's Whipple-Scrumptious Fudgemallow Delight chocolate bars. Charlie ripped open the wrapper.

There was no Golden Ticket to be seen, but Charlie happily gobbled down the bar. He loved it so much that he decided to buy just one more.

He tore off the wrapper on the second bar and suddenly saw a bright flash of gold.

"It's a Golden Ticket!" screamed the shopkeeper, leaping about a foot into the air. "You've found the last Golden Ticket!"

The Golden Ticket looked like a piece of pure gold that had been pounded down to the thinness of paper. The writing on the ticket said, "Tremendous things are in store for you!

Many wonderful surprises await you! For now, I do invite you to come to my factory and be my guest for one whole day. . . . The day I have chosen for the visit is the first day in the month of February. . . . And you are allowed to bring with you either one or two members of your own family to look after you and to ensure that you don't get into mischief."

On the first day of February, Charlie and his grandpa Joe stood outside the iron gates of Wonka's factory. Standing next to them were the four other children who had found Golden Tickets, their parents, and a huge crowd of onlookers. At ten o'clock, as the town's church bells started ringing, the gates slowly swung open.

A Geographical Mystery

In *Charlie and the Chocolate Factory*, Roald Dahl chose not to reveal the names of the towns, cities, or countries where Charlie or Willy Wonka or any of the characters lived. For example, all we learn about Veruca Salt is that she came from "a great city far away." One clue to Charlie's location was that he found a dollar bill in the snow. Did that mean that Charlie was an American or Australian? Not necessarily. In the British edition of the book, Charlie found a fifty-pence coin. Readers never did find out where Wonka's factory was actually located.

Someone shouted, "*There he is! That's him!*" And sure enough. Willy Wonka was standing there, just beyond the open gates. The children— and readers everywhere—were about to meet this remarkable man.

CHAPTER 5
Willy Wonka

Roald Dahl described Willy Wonka as "an extraordinary little man," and that was certainly true.

Willy Wonka wore a tall black hat and a long coat made of plum-colored velvet. His pants were green, his gloves were gray, and he carried a long walking stick that was topped with gold.

"Covering his chin, there was a small, neat, pointed black beard—a goatee. And his eyes—his eyes were most marvelously bright. They seemed to be sparkling and twinkling at you all the time. The whole face, in fact, was alight with fun and laughter."

Instead of walking, he did a "funny little

skipping dance." Willy Wonka was "like a squirrel in the quickness of his movements."

Grandpa Joe had described him this way: "Mr. Willy Wonka is the most *amazing*, the most *fantastic*, the most *extraordinary* chocolate maker the world has ever seen! . . . He's a *magician* with chocolate! He can make *anything*—anything he wants!"

Willy Wonka had invented more than two hundred types of chocolate bars, each with a different center. He had created ice cream that didn't melt for many hours, even if it was left out in the sun. He made chewing gum that never lost its flavor.

One time, Willy Wonka even created an entire palace made out of chocolate for an Indian prince named Pondicherry. The palace was constructed using chocolate bricks, with chocolate cement holding them in place, and all the walls, ceilings, rugs, furniture, and beds were made of chocolate. When the prince turned on his bathroom faucets, hot chocolate came flowing out.

The Other Mister Wonka

In 1971, Roald Dahl received a letter from a man named Bill Wonka, who lived in Nebraska. He complained that Roald had used his name without permission! Roald wrote back to Bill Wonka and explained that Roald's half brother Louis had come up with the Wonka name when they were children. Louis invented a boomerang-like toy that he called a Skilly Wonka.

The children and adults on the tour soon
discovered that the Wonka Factory was almost as
amazing as Willy Wonka himself. The first stop
on the tour was the Chocolate Room. This was a

beautiful and immense valley with green meadows
on both sides and an unusual brown river flowing
between them. A waterfall thundered over a cliff
and poured into the brown river.

"It's *all* chocolate!" declared Willy Wonka. "Every drop of that river is hot melted chocolate of the finest quality. The *very* finest quality. There's enough chocolate in there to fill *every* bathtub in the *entire* country! *And* all the swimming pools as well! Thousands of gallons an hour, my dear children! Thousands and thousands of gallons!"

The children and their parents were even more astonished when they met Willy Wonka's new factory employees. The workers were an extraordinary group of little people called Oompa-Loompas. Years ago, Wonka explained, he had rescued the Oompa-Loompas from a dangerous jungle where they had been threatened by horrible creatures such as hornswogglers and snozzwangers and whangdoodles. After Willy Wonka sent all his former employees home, the Oompa-Loompas replaced them and became full-time workers at the factory.

The children also visited the Inventing Room, where Wonka was developing Everlasting Gobstoppers. That was a new and top-secret candy that could be sucked for hours without ever growing smaller. Among the many fantastic candies the children saw during their tour were "eatable marshmallow pillows," lickable wallpaper, and hot ice cream for cold days.

Willy Wonka had a sense of humor, but he also had a darker side. When some of the children on the tour misbehaved and found themselves in danger, Wonka seemed more concerned about possible damage to his factory.

Augustus Gloop disobeyed Willy Wonka's warning not to touch the chocolate river, and then the boy tumbled into the river and was sucked into the pipes beneath its surface.

Violet Beauregarde chewed a stick of gum that caused her to puff up and turn as blue as a blueberry. Veruca Salt tried to steal a squirrel that was shelling nuts in a factory room, and as a result, found herself tossed down a garbage chute. And Mike Teavee was zapped by a special type of television camera that shrank him to a height of just one inch.

As the four misbehaving children disappeared one by one from the tour, Willy Wonka continued to dart down the hallways of his factory.

"Come on!" he declared. "Hurry up! We *must* get going! And how many children are there left now?"

He quickly discovered that Charlie was the only one, and this caused Willy Wonka to explode with happiness and excitement.

"But my *dear boy*," he cried out, "*that means you've won*! Oh, I do congratulate you! I'm absolutely delighted! How wonderful this is! Well *done*, Charlie, well *done*! Now the fun is really going to start! But we mustn't dilly! We mustn't dally! We have an *enormous* number of things to do before the day is out!"

Willy Wonka quickly guided Charlie and Grandpa Joe into a fantastic glass elevator that traveled up, down, and sideways. The elevator shot up and through the roof of the factory and zoomed through the air toward Charlie's house. Wonka explained that the elevator was able to fly thanks to "candy power."

It was during this journey that Willy Wonka revealed his biggest surprise yet. He was going to give his entire chocolate factory to Charlie!

"As soon as you are old enough to run it, the entire factory will become yours," said Wonka.

After the whole Bucket family was invited to the factory and then loaded into the glass elevator, Charlie happily told his parents and grandparents that they were all going to live in "the most wonderful place in the world!"

Charlie's Grandma Josephine nervously asked if there would be anything to eat at the factory.

"Anything to *eat*?" cried Charlie, laughing. "Oh, you just wait and see!"

CHAPTER 6
Books and Screenplays

Charlie and the Chocolate Factory was first published in the United States in 1964. It quickly became Roald Dahl's most successful book, selling over 600,000 copies in the United States in just three years!

Even though the book was a big hit in the United States, it took three years for Roald to find a British publisher willing to release *Charlie and the Chocolate Factory* in England. Over eleven publishers in England turned it down. It was thanks to Roald's daughter Tessa that *Charlie* finally found a British publisher. She gave a copy

of the American edition of *James and the Giant Peach* to one of her school friends. That friend was a girl named Camilla Unwin, and she was the daughter of a British publisher named Rayner Unwin. Mr. Unwin decided to publish British editions of both *James* and *Charlie* in 1967. Within a few weeks, all copies of both were sold out.

Rayner Unwin and *The Hobbit*

The British book publisher Rayner Unwin (1925–2000) showed a talent for discovering successful children's books long before he published Roald Dahl's books. When Rayner was only ten years old, he had read a manuscript of J. R. R. Tolkien's *The Hobbit*. Rayner gave it to his father, who was a partner at a British publishing company, George Allen & Unwin Ltd. of London. They took young Rayner's advice and published the first edition of *The Hobbit* in 1937.

With *Charlie and the Chocolate Factory* a big success in America and Europe, Roald wrote a

couple of screenplays. One was for *You Only Live Twice*, a 1967 movie adaptation of a James Bond spy novel written by Ian Fleming. The movie was a big hit, and Roald followed it up with a screenplay for a 1968 movie musical called *Chitty Chitty Bang Bang*. The original children's book that inspired this movie had also been written by Ian Fleming.

One of the most memorable characters in the *Chitty Chitty Bang Bang* movie did not appear in Fleming's original book but was instead created by Roald Dahl. That was the incredibly evil

Child Catcher. This monstrous villain had a long and very sensitive nose, which he used to sniff and locate children in their hiding places.

The Child Catcher used candy to attract the attention of children and then capture them. In almost every way, the Child Catcher was the opposite of Willy Wonka!

Ian Fleming (1908–1964)

Ian Fleming was a British author, journalist, and naval intelligence officer during World War II. After the war, Fleming used his experience working as a spy to create his most famous literary character.

This was secret agent James Bond, also known as Agent 007. Fleming wrote fourteen best-selling James Bond novels, and Bond's introductory phrase, "Bond, James Bond," became known all around the world. All his Bond books and his only children's book, *Chitty Chitty Bang Bang: The Magical Car*, were made into movies.

Roald Dahl next wrote a children's book called *Fantastic Mr. Fox*. It was published in 1970 and quickly became a best seller. It told the tale of a smart-thinking fox who outwitted three evil farmers who were causing trouble for Mr. Fox's family and friends.

The early 1970s also saw the appearance of a brand-new version of Willy Wonka. Six years after Willy Wonka made his publishing debut, the character was about to make a big impression on movie screens around the world.

CHAPTER 7
Willy Wonka Becomes a Movie Star

In 1970, Roald Dahl was hired to write a screenplay for a movie version of *Charlie and the Chocolate Factory.* The producer of the movie wasn't happy with Roald's screenplay, and another writer was hired to alter it. The movie became a musical, and it had a new title: *Willy Wonka & the Chocolate Factory.* That was only the first of many changes made to Roald's original story.

Along with songs created for several of the characters, new plot points were developed for

Wonka's rival, Arthur Slugworth

the movie, including the death of Charlie's father and a job for Charlie working as a newspaper delivery boy. Another change made for the movie was to show Willy Wonka's biggest rival in the chocolate business. This was a man named Arthur Slugworth, and he tried to bribe all five children on the tour to steal a sample of Wonka's not-yet-released Everlasting Gobstoppers candy.

Three of the movie's bratty children—Augustus Gloop, Violet Beauregarde, and Mike Teavee— met the same dreadful outcomes as in Dahl's book. The movie's Veruca Salt had a different story.

In the book, Veruca ran into problems with some squirrels shelling nuts in the factory. In the movie, she has a tantrum in the Golden Eggs Room. When she steps onto a giant scale, Veruca is tossed down a garbage chute.

"She was a bad egg," concluded Willy Wonka.

"The Candy Man"

Bill, the owner of a candy store in the movie *Willy Wonka & the Chocolate Factory*, appeared in only a few scenes. But he got to sing the movie's hit song, "The Candy Man," including these lyrics:

> *Willy Wonka makes*
> *Everything he bakes*
> *Satisfying and delicious*
> *Talk about your childhood wishes*
> *You can even eat the dishes!*

The song was very popular, and it eventually became a number one hit for the singer Sammy Davis Jr.

The famous comedy actor Gene Wilder was cast in the role of Willy Wonka. Before he accepted the role, he told the producer of the movie that he had one requirement: "When I make my first entrance, I'd like to come out of the door carrying a cane and then walk toward the crowd with a limp. . . . They all whisper to themselves and then

become deathly quiet. As I walk toward them, my cane sinks into one of the cobblestones I'm walking on and stands straight up, by itself; but I keep on walking, until I realize that I no longer have my cane. I start to fall forward, and just before I hit the ground, I do a beautiful forward somersault and bounce back up, to great applause."

Gene Wilder (1933–2016)

Gene Wilder was a talented actor, writer, director, producer and singer/songwriter. He was born Jerome Silberman in Milwaukee, Wisconsin. He got his start acting onstage and made his big screen debut in the 1967 movie *Bonnie and Clyde*. He followed that up with starring roles in movies he made with his friend Mel Brooks, including the comedy classics *Blazing Saddles* and *Young Frankenstein*. Gene Wilder also co-wrote *Young Frankenstein*. He went on to star in many more movies in the 1980s and 1990s.

Wilder received an Emmy award for his last acting performance, which was on the TV show *Will & Grace* in 2003.

Perhaps the biggest change made for the movie was that Charlie and Grandpa Joe misbehaved during the factory tour by secretly sampling Wonka's Fizzy Lifting Drinks. At the end of the tour, an outraged Willy Wonka yelled at them, "You stole Fizzy Lifting Drinks. So you get *nothing*! You *lose*!"

Grandpa Joe angrily responded, "You're an inhuman monster!"

At the end of the movie, though, everything worked out just as it had in the book. Charlie promised that he would never reveal the secrets of the Everlasting Gobstoppers candy to Wonka's rival Slugworth. Willy Wonka forgave Charlie for

his misbehavior and still handed over control of the factory to him.

Willy Wonka & the Chocolate Factory was not a big success in 1971, but it grew in popularity over the years as it was shown on television and reissued in home video formats. Today it is a beloved classic.

CHAPTER 8
The Further Adventures
of Willy Wonka

Roald Dahl decided to write a sequel to *Charlie and the Chocolate Factory*. It was called *Charlie and the Great Glass Elevator*, and it was published in the United States in 1972.

The new book continued the story exactly from where the first book ended. The whole chocolate factory had been promised to Charlie Bucket. He and his entire family were crammed into Willy Wonka's wonderful glass elevator as it soared through the air and headed back to the factory.

Unfortunately, through a series of mistakes, the elevator didn't make it to the factory and instead sailed far above Earth.

Roald Dahl wrote, "Higher and higher rushed the Great Glass Elevator until soon they could see the countries and oceans of the earth spread out below them like a map."

Charlie's grandmother screamed in fright, and Charlie asked Willy Wonka if they had gone too far.

"Too *far*?" responded Wonka. "I'll say we went too far! You know where we've gone, my friends? We've gone into orbit!"

The Space Race

During the 1950s and 1960s, there was a "space race" between the United States and the Soviet Union to see which country would be the first to achieve several spaceflight milestones. In 1961, President John F. Kennedy pledged that the United States would land a man on the moon by the end of the decade. That remarkable event occurred in 1969.

Three years later, when *Charlie and the Great Glass Elevator* was published, five more crewed spaceships had landed on the moon. It seemed that everyone was talking about outer space and the possibilities of space travel!

It turned out that the glass elevator wasn't the only thing orbiting Earth in the second book. There was also a new satellite in outer space that belonged to the United States. This giant satellite was called Space Hotel "U.S.A." and it was an ultradeluxe hotel where guests would arrive via rocket ship. Willy Wonka landed the elevator at the entrance to the hotel, and soon the whole gang entered the satellite.

The Space Hotel was not yet open for business, though, and back on Earth, the president of the United States and all the members of his cabinet were upset to learn that Willy Wonka and the Bucket family had wandered into the hotel!

Even worse, Wonka and the Buckets soon discovered that the hotel was overrun with large and very dangerous monsters from outer space. These strange creatures were known as Vermicious Knids, and they looked like large, greenish-brown eggs balanced on their pointy ends.

Vermicious Knids

Willy Wonka knew all about these monsters and said, "The Vermicious Knid can turn itself into any shape it wants. It has no bones. Its body is really one huge muscle, enormously strong, but very stretchy and squishy, like a mixture of rubber and putty with steel wires inside. . . . From fifty yards away, a fully grown Vermicious Knid could stretch out its neck and bite your head off without even getting up! . . . These Vermicious Knids are the terror of the Universe. They travel through space in great swarms, landing on other stars and planets and destroying everything they find."

Willy Wonka and the Buckets scrambled back into the Glass Elevator, only to be pursued by thousands of Vermicious Knids. As the elevator streaked downward toward Earth, Willy Wonka suddenly remembered what happens to a Vermicious Knid when it enters Earth's atmosphere at high speed.

"He gets red-hot," Wonka said. "He burns away in a long fiery trail. Soon these dirty beasts will start popping like popcorn!"

Sure enough, that is exactly what happened. As the elevator approached Earth, the Vermicious Knids began to sizzle and heat up. Then suddenly, the monsters became white-hot and exploded.

"What a splendid sight," said Wonka. "It's better than fireworks."

There were a few more complications back at the chocolate factory, including two of Charlie's grandparents being turned into babies after they drank a formula called Wonka-Vite that subtracted eighty years each from their ages. Another of Charlie's grandparents drank way too much

of the formula and vanished altogether! Thanks to some quick thinking by Charlie, Willy Wonka gave them doses of Vita-Wonk, and all three grandparents were restored to their actual ages.

With all the problems sorted out, everyone received an invitation to a big party at the White House. There, the US president planned to pin medals of bravery on Willy Wonka and all others in the Bucket family.

The final sentences spoken in the book by Willy Wonka were warm words of praise for young Charlie, who would be inheriting the Wonka Factory.

"Charlie!" cried Mr. Wonka. "What *would* we do without you? You're brilliant!"

The Movie That Never Was

After *Charlie and the Great Glass Elevator* was published, Roald Dahl received a request from the producers of the *Willy Wonka & the Chocolate Factory* movie. They asked if they could make a film of the new book. But Roald hadn't been happy with the 1971 movie. And he turned down the idea for a sequel.

CHAPTER 9
Final Books

After *Charlie and the Great Glass Elevator*, Roald Dahl wrote many more books, including a memoir called *Boy: Tales of Childhood*. In that book, he revealed all the details of "The Great Mouse Plot" and other stories about his happy days with his family and his awful boarding school experiences. He also wrote a book called *Going Solo* about his time as a military pilot.

In 1978, Roald had started working on a third *Charlie* book, which he planned to call *Charlie in the White House*. The new book was going to pick up right where *Charlie and the Great Glass Elevator* ended. Unfortunately, Roald completed only the first chapter of the book.

During the 1980s, Roald wrote three children's books that became classics: *The BFG* was published in 1982, *The Witches* in 1983, and *Matilda* in 1988. Each of the three books was later made into a movie.

Charlie in the White House

The first chapter from this unfinished book can be seen at the Roald Dahl Museum and Story Centre in the village of Great Missenden in Buckinghamshire, England. Roald lived in this village for the last thirty-six years of his life. In the one chapter of the book, the president of the United States is standing on the

White House lawn next to members of his cabinet, including the Director of Sewage and Garbage Disposal and the Director of Public Relations and Bamboozlement. They are all awaiting the arrival of the Bucket family and Willy Wonka after their adventures in outer space.

The Roald Dahl Museum is the only place you can find this tiny bit of the book that never was.

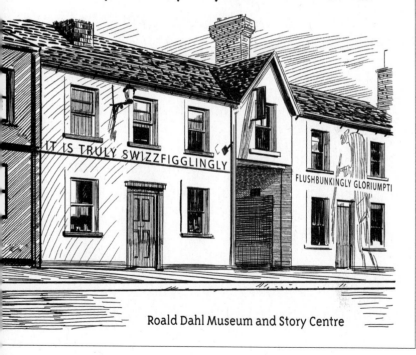

Roald Dahl Museum and Story Centre

It was estimated a few years ago that Roald Dahl's books have sold over three hundred million copies worldwide. They have been translated into sixty-three languages, including Bulgarian, Icelandic, and Vietnamese.

As for *Charlie and the Chocolate Factory*, it continues to be a best seller around the world, becoming more popular than ever. When the

book was published in China in 2009, it had a print run of two million copies, the most for any book in China at that time.

Roald Dahl died in 1990, at the age of seventy-four. He never got to finish his third *Charlie* book, but it turned out that there was still some life left in his character of Willy Wonka.

CHAPTER 10
A New Movie

In 2005, Willy Wonka returned to the big screen in a new film called *Charlie and the Chocolate Factory*. It starred Johnny Depp in the role of Willy Wonka and was directed by Tim Burton.

Johnny Depp and Tim Burton

As in 1971, the moviemakers decided to make some changes to Roald Dahl's original story. In the new movie, it turned out that Grandpa Joe used to work at Willy Wonka's factory, and Violet Beauregarde was a martial arts champion. A woman offered Charlie $500 for his Golden Ticket, and he even considered selling it to her.

Charlie Bucket from Tim Burton's *Charlie and the Chocolate Factory*

"We need the money more than we need the chocolate," Charlie sadly told his family.

Tim Burton (1958–)

American director, writer, and artist Tim Burton got his start working on animated cartoons for Walt Disney Studios. He directed the 1988 hit movie *Beetlejuice*, and the following year he directed *Batman*, which became one of the biggest hits in Hollywood history. Other popular movies directed by Burton include *Pee-Wee's Big Adventure*, *Edward Scissorhands*, *The Nightmare Before Christmas*, *Alice in Wonderland*, *Frankenweenie*, and *Dark Shadows*.

Fortunately, Charlie's family convinced him to tour the chocolate factory, accompanied by his beloved Grandpa Joe.

The biggest change made for the movie was to reveal a new story about Willy Wonka's sad childhood. The filmmakers added the character of his father, Dr. Wilbur Wonka, the city's most famous dentist. Wilbur was a very stern parent who strongly disapproved of *all* sweets.

Wilbur Wonka in a scene from Tim Burton's
Charlie and the Chocolate Factory

One Halloween, he took away all young Willy Wonka's candy and declared, "Candy is a waste of time! No son of mine is going to be a chocolatier."

"Then I'll run away," cried Willy Wonka, "to Switzerland . . . Bavaria . . . the candy capitals of the world!"

Young Willy Wonka did indeed leave home, vowing never to see his father again. Even after Willy Wonka opened his chocolate factory many years later, he still refused to contact his father.

There was another big change made to Roald Dahl's original story. At the end of the tour in the movie, Charlie was the last child standing, as in all the other versions of the story. But in this new movie, Willy Wonka told Charlie that he was not allowed to bring his family to live with him in the chocolate factory!

"Look at me," Willy Wonka explained to Charlie. "I had no family, and I'm a giant success."

But Charlie refused to leave his parents and grandparents behind.

"I wouldn't give up my family for anything," declared Charlie. "Not for all the chocolate in the world."

A surprised Willy Wonka responded, "Wow. Well, that's just unexpected. And weird."

In the end, Charlie helped Willy Wonka restore the relationship with his father. This time, there were two happy endings to the story: one for the Bucket family and another for Willy Wonka and *his* family.

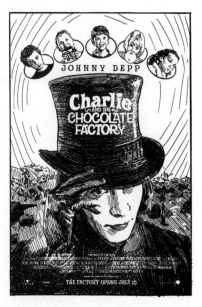

The Difficult Job of Being an Oompa-Loompa

In the 1971 movie *Willy Wonka & the Chocolate Factory*, many little people portrayed the Oompa-Loompas. For the 2005 film *Charlie and the Chocolate Factory*, director Tim Burton decided that only one person would be cast as an Oompa-Loompa. All the other Oompa-Loompas would be exact clones of that actor. The filmmakers hired an actor named Deep Roy,

Deep Roy

and they then used CGI (computer-generated imagery) to transform him into hundreds of Oompa-Loompas. To play many different Oompa-Loompas, Deep Roy had to do stunts, dance, sing, play musical instruments, and even learn how to climb a mountain. "I think he had the hardest job in the movie," said Burton.

CHAPTER 11
Willy Wonka Forever

Was it any surprise to learn that Willy Wonka had a few more tricks up his very purple sleeves?

In 2013, he starred in a stage musical called *Charlie and the Chocolate Factory* that premiered in London. Four years later, the show moved to a Broadway theater in New York City. A British actor named Douglas Hodge played Willy Wonka in London, and Christian Borle performed the role in New York.

Marc Shaiman and Scott Wittman, who had found success with their musical *Hairspray*, wrote the new show's music and lyrics. When they started working on *Charlie and the Chocolate Factory*, the two men decided that none of the songs from the two movies would be included in the stage show. Eventually, though, they did add two songs from the 1971 film, "Pure Imagination" and "The Candy Man," to their score.

Scott Wittman and Marc Shaiman

The plot of the musical followed the original story of the book fairly closely, although there were a few updates. Veruca Salt became a rap star with her own television show. And Mike Teavee spent all his time playing video games.

The show received mostly good reviews in London, but the producers decided to make a number of changes for the Broadway production. The revised show opened in New York City in 2017 but was not a big success. It closed the following year.

But even that wasn't the end of Willy Wonka and his wonderful adventures.

Two *Charlie and the Chocolate Factory* video games were produced, one in 1985 and another in 2005.

The book inspired an amusement park ride at the Alton Towers theme park in Staffordshire, England. During the ride, visitors traveled around the chocolate factory in bright pink boats on

a chocolate river. In the final stage of the ride, the guests joined Willy Wonka in a glass elevator and traveled up and through the roof of the factory.

There was even an opera called *The Golden Ticket* that had its world premiere in St. Louis, Missouri, in 2010. The  cartoon cat and mouse team of Tom and Jerry starred in a 2017 video called *Tom and Jerry: Willy Wonka & the Chocolate Factory*.

Most recently, Netflix announced that it is working on a new animated series based on the original book. So we can probably expect to see more and more of Willy Wonka in the coming years.

As Roald Dahl wrote, in the very last sentence of *Charlie and the Great Glass Elevator*: "It's not over yet," Charlie said, laughing. "It hasn't even begun."

Bibliography

*Books for young readers

*Boothroyd, Jennifer. *Roald Dahl: A Life of Imagination.* Minneapolis, MN: Lerner Publications, 2008.

*Cooling, Wendy. *D Is for Dahl: A Gloriumptious A–Z Guide to the World of Roald Dahl.* New York: Puffin Books, 2004.

*Dahl, Roald. *Boy: Tales of Childhood.* New York: Puffin Books, 2009.

*Dahl, Roald. *The Complete Adventures of Charlie and Mr. Willy Wonka.* New York: Puffin Books, 2010.

*Kelley, True. *Who Was Roald Dahl?* New York: Penguin Workshop, 2012.

Sturrock, Donald. *Storyteller: The Authorized Biography of Roald Dahl.* New York: Simon & Schuster, 2010.

Treglown, Jeremy. *Roald Dahl: A Biography.* New York: Farrar Straus Giroux, 1994.

Timeline of Willy Wonka

1916 | **1964** | **1967** | **1971** | **1972** | **1985** | **1990** | **2005** | **2006** | **2010** | **2013** | **2017** | **2020**

Roald Dahl is born on September 13 in Cardiff, Wales

Charlie and the Chocolate Factory is published in England

Charlie and the Chocolate Factory is published in the United States

Charlie and the Great Glass Elevator is published

The first *Charlie and the Chocolate Factory* video game is released

The movie *Charlie and the Chocolate Factory* comes out

An opera adaptation of *Charlie and the Chocolate Factory* called *The Golden Ticket* opens in St. Louis, Missouri

The revised stage musical *Charlie and the Chocolate Factory* opens in New York City

The stage musical *Charlie and the Chocolate Factory* opens in London

The British theme park Alton Towers opens a ride based on *Charlie and the Chocolate Factory*

The movie *Willy Wonka & the Chocolate Factory* is released

Roald Dahl dies on November 23

A *Charlie and the Chocolate Factory* video game based on the 2005 movie is released

Netflix begins development on a new animated series based on *Charlie and the Chocolate Factory*